HAPPIER
IN THE
COUNTRY

HAPPIER
IN THE
COUNTRY

Jane Reed Lennon

Illustrated by Ellen Oliver Parsons

PROSPECT HILL

Baltimore, Maryland

Tools first appeared in
Green Scene magazine, May 1987

Library of Congress Catalog Card Number 87-61162

ISBN 0-941526-04-6

PROSPECT HILL
216 Wendover Road
Baltimore, Maryland, 21218

Dedicated to Jean Byrne

CONTENTS

HAPPIER
IN THE
COUNTRY

This Sweet Spot

I have always known this farm. It belonged to various relatives for many years. Though I was raised in a rural area, we referred to this property as the country. It was used as a summer place or a weekend retreat and we visited and picnicked here, but for fifty years there was no year-round resident and no farmer.

I always knew this sweet spot, but I never dreamed I'd own it! When we were offered the chance to buy this farm, it was like dropping something big into a still pool. The ripples go out and out from the center and rock everything in the pond—the fish, the mud, the bugs, the weeds, even the reflected sunlight. Buying the farm was like that. It rocked and shook our lives. It changed us around, and when the dust settled here we were—my husband Patrick, our four-year old son Pierre, and I—on the farm in the country.

To celebrate buying the farm, I made a huge cookie that

was really a gingerbread map of the farm with white cookie dough marking the lanes, the house, the barn, and the boundaries. This is not a large farm. It covers the south side of a ridge from one road at the top to another road at the bottom. Our farmstead is on a level spot right in the middle of the hillside. We cannot see a road, or traffic, or any other house from here.

The little eighteenth-century house sits on top of a spring of fresh water. It is sheltered from the winds by the hillside rising up behind it to the northwest. The low winter sun shines across a distant ridge and into our windows. We are always reminded of the skill of the early settlers in choosing sites for their buildings. This spot has water, good winter light, and good air drainage, which means that the cold air, always moving to the lowest place, does not stop here on the hillside but flows into the valley below. The farmyard is sheltered from the winds that blow hard from the west.

Small fields are scattered over the hillside. Long before our time all the relatively level areas were cleared, and the stones were piled into walls surrounding the fields. Once people grew tobacco, blueberries, oats, potatoes, corn, and other vegetables in the small fields, but when we came here all the old fields had grown into woods.

The farm was ours! We walked around and around our hillside making lists. We figured we were not likely to have nothing to do for about forty years. As we walked and looked, talked and explored, we decided two things. First, we would try to look at each part of the farm at least once a week because we were now the stewards of the land. Second, we would need a good map, one more exact than the cookie map of our celebration.

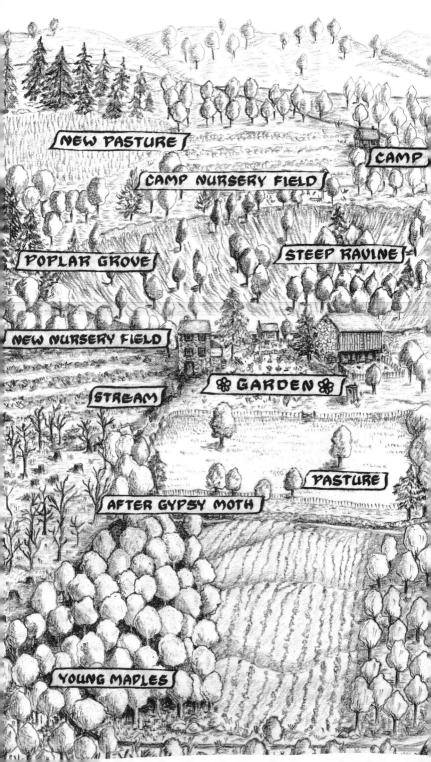

NEW PASTURE

CAMP

CAMP NURSERY FIELD

POPLAR GROVE

STEEP RAVINE

NEW NURSERY FIELD

❀ GARDEN ❀

STREAM

PASTURE

AFTER GYPSY MOTH

YOUNG MAPLES

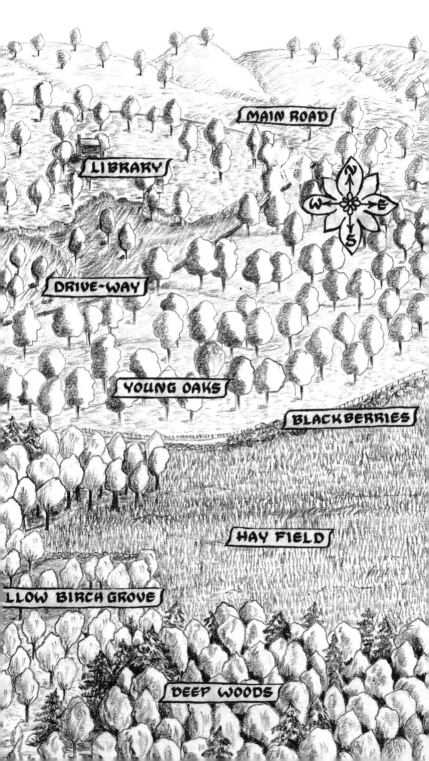

Getting Started

Five years ago, on Midsummer's Day we moved into our Pennsylvania farm. We have beaten back the woods and let the sunshine in. We have repaired and reroofed our beautiful stone buildings. We have cleared off and leveled lawn areas, re-stacked dry stone walls, and made steps and ramps to connect the terraced levels. We have drained the soggy ground. We have put tons and tons of stones into the driveway and moved tons of soil to make raised beds for our perennial nursery.

Both Patrick and I grew up in the country. We both thought we knew what we would have to do and how we would do it to make this place functional. We didn't! We are lucky to have brought a certain amount of knowledge and skill with us. But neither of us had any idea when we arrived here just what would be involved in making a derelict vacation spot into a viable farm.

It's a good thing we didn't know. If we had given it

clearer and more careful thought, we might never have come.

Patrick is good with tools. He can build, rebuild, make, or fix almost anything. As soon as we cleared the driveway and could get into the barn, Patrick set up his workshop there.

I am good at growing things. I was raised by two gardeners and I studied horticulture at home, in school, and as an apprentice gardener. At my childhood home we always had farm animals in large or small numbers, so I am also the keeper of the animals.

We are all of us great readers, which has been essential to our life here—for entertainment, inspiration, and information. If we don't know something, we get the book!

We brought our tools, books, and knowledge here with us. I quit my job. Patrick closed his photography studio. Pierre dropped out of infant school. We sold our house, paid for the farm, and arrived here full of hope and excitement, flat broke.

We have known lots of people who have "gone back to the land." Most of them move back to town or return to a nine-to-five suburban life when their savings are depleted. We didn't have any savings. We had already spent every cent we could gather together buying the farm.

We considered borrowing money but found, not surprisingly, that bankers don't lend money to people with no money and no jobs. Looking back, we are glad about that. If we had borrowed, we would be in debt, which is much more expensive than being broke.

During that first summer we explored and made lists and worked in the farmyard area around the house and barn. We had the County Extension Agent come to see the farm and pumped him for advice and ideas. We also had the District Forester come, since most of this farm is wooded. Both of these people, the Extension Agent and the District Forester, are public officials. Their jobs are to give people free advice and guidance on how to use the natural resources of their property.

The Forester was especially helpful to us because we had no idea how to manage our huge areas of wooded land. Together with the Forester, we identified the different kinds of trees and areas of woodland. Each area was numbered or named, and identified on a map of the whole property. The Forester suggested that we work on one area, and only one area, for five years and then move on to the next area.

We decided that our first forestry project should be an eleven-acre woods where mature trees had been heavily damaged by gypsy moths. This area needed to be harvested, cleaned up, and re-planted. The other eight areas were ranked according to tree size and need for attention.

To the west and north of our house is a poplar grove. The trees were already large, straight, and tall when we moved. The Forester, looking at the tulip poplars and then down at little four-year-old Pierre, suggested that the poplar grove be area number three. In fifteen years the poplars would be prime timber and would help pay for Pierre's college education.

Having the Forester helped put our whole project into perspective. A farm isn't an object; it's a living, growing, changing place. Things don't get done overnight. We are here for the long haul. Forty years from now, when the eleven-acre woods needs our attention again, we will still be here to harvest the trees we planted this spring.

A Farm

A farm is a piece of land being used by people to grow something that yields an income. Land used wisely pays for itself, pays the expenses of ownership, and pays the farmer for his work.

A farmer has to know the land in order to make decisions about its use. In our area farmland consists of three main types. Tillable land, relatively level and fertile, is farmland where crops are planted, grown, and harvested by the farmer. Rough, rocky, hilly, or wet lands are used for pasture. Farm animals graze there during the warm weather, eating the grasses and brush. The third type of land is woodland. The forested parts of a farm provide windbreaks and shelter for wildlife, and hold water and soil on the hillsides, preventing erosion. In addition, woodland is productive. Logs are harvested for lumber; dead wood is used for firewood; and pulp wood is sold for papermaking.

The farmer has to know the land to decide which crops to grow; which animals to raise, and how many; and which trees to harvest. And the farmer has to take care of the land. Each crop harvested takes something from the land, and this must be replaced. The farmer, in addition to planting, growing, and harvesting, is always responsible for improving the land. If this is neglected, the land becomes less and less produtive.

The land we bought was not a farm because it did not produce anything to yield an income. When we decided to buy the farm, we realized that we would have to put it into production, growing crops that would yield an income. We would have to work to support the farm, and we hoped that it would soon pay us for farming.

We decided to have a flower farm, a nursery, growing perennial flower plants. Growing and selling young flower plants would make good use of our small fields and hilly land, and it was something we already knew quite a lot about before we moved to the farm.

After a great deal of thought and discussion, we decided to have a wholesale business. We would acquire plants, propogate and increase them, clear and develop nursery ground, and establish our market. Since we live close to a number of horticulturally active urban centers, we would be able to solicit business from the many garden designers and landscape services in our area.

The nursery would occupy only a small part of our total acreage. Careful management of the woodland would pay our real estate taxes and insurance. All expenditures would be weighed against returns. Farm equipment and land improvement would have precedence over people comforts. A tractor would pay for itself, indoor plumbing would not. Anything we *could* live without, we *would* live without until the farm was launched.

Flowers by the Armload

We never run out of flowers. From early March until late November we are surrounded by garden flowers. During the snow-covered months we have potted flowers on the deep windowsills of our house to brighten the rooms and our spirits.

There are always flowers here to cut and sell, and we dry flowers to make into wreaths and everlasting bouquets. There is always an armload of flowers to send home with any visitor. We give flowers to schools, churches, or service groups that ask for them, and we take flowers to people when we visit.

Our gardens and nursery grounds are filled with a changing pattern of colors and lovely flowery shapes. As one variety fades and finishes its seasonal show, it is replaced by another. We never run out of flowers.

The remains of an old garden were here when we came to the farm. The toughest of garden pernnials had held their ground among the grasses, weeds, wildflowers, and trees that grew up around them. Old fashioned single-flowered peonies, sweet fragrant German iris, yuccas with sword-like leaves and six-foot flower spikes, and thousands of daffodils competed with a green tide.

Along the stream and in the wet meadow, blue, purple, and white Siberian iris made drifts of color in June. Later great blue lobelia and yellow day lilies spangled the grass. There were violets of every description—purple ones, sweet white violets, trailing yellow violets, rose-colored ones, speckled ones, and pale gray Confederate violets.

One large hillside area was completely covered with hostas. Their big, ribbed, bright green leaves overlapped to cover the rocky ground, and in late July each clump gave rise to a tall stem of fragrant purple bells. Several enormous patches of hydrangea, with fat white snowball blossoms, covered another steep bank. Old fashioned roses, hidden in the green jungle, showed themselves in June when their lovely flowers appeared.

There were flowering dogwoods, bush honeysuckles, quinces with bright red-orange blossoms, and lilacs, all grown over and tangled with wild grape and briars. Columbines, red, blue, and rose-colored ones, appeared in odd places. Sedums grew from walls and rock piles, and huge patches of mint and beebalm grew around the springhouse door.

We worked slowly through this horticultural treasure house, watching and waiting to see what would appear. Our long garden evolved from the remnants of the old garden. Many plants were moved and hundreds of new ones added. The thin soil in the old garden has been enriched, and the shrubs have been pruned and untangled. Everything has prospered with this attention.

The blissful garden changes from day to day, and each year it is different as its many varieties of plants grow and increase or occasionally die out. It nourishes our souls. We never run out of flowers.

A Beeline

A neighbor came by to say hello. The farm chat went over the weather (cold) and the lambs at his farm (seventeen so far) and got around to bees. He inquired about our bees, so we walked out to the hive to check on them.

The bee box was undisturbed on its stand, the tiny doorway facing south. The beehive looked fine.

The neighbor put his ear to the bee box and listened for a long time. "They are dead," he said. Then he added:

> *"Bees in May is worth a load of hay*
> *Bees in June is none to soon*
> *Bees in July is sure to die."*

Our bees had come from a big old cherry tree along the driveway. During a downpour thunderstorm in August, a large dead branch, full of honey, honeycomb, and bees, had broken off and fallen to the ground, leaving the remainer of the broken hive in the standing stump.

Their home was ruined! We kept away from the bees and called Robert, the bee man. He arrived with stands, boxes, frames, and bee gear. There are certain people who love bees and know just how to deal with them. The bees seem to feel this and the bee man can touch the bees, move among them, even take their honey, and the bees don't sting him, or even fuss much.

We sat on the hillside above the broken hive and watched the bee man patiently moving hundreds of bees and piles of honey to a new hive by the stump. When he had them more or less moved, he left them to sort things out for themselves.

Later, in the dark of night when the bees had calmed down, we moved the beehive to an open grassy spot east of the barnyard.

Because of the loss of their honey and the structure of their hive, and the loss of so many eggs and bee larvae when their old home was wrecked, we gave the bees sugar syrup from special feeders. The remaining bees also foraged in the fields of asters and goldenrod, but it was not enough.

In an established beehive, bees generate enough body heat to prevent freezing, but our hive had too few bees. During a period of really intense cold, the weakened community of bees froze.

We had enjoyed watching the bees during the fall. We

saw how the expressions "busy as a bee" and "make a beeline" came into use. One day a beeline went straight into the summer kitchen. I had cooked a huge quantity of elderberries and poured all the juicy pulp into a cloth sack. The juice was dripping out of this jelly sack into a big pot to be made into elderberry jelly. When I came in from my garden to check on the juice, the whole summer kitchen was dark and loud with honeybees.

Because we are not bee people, we knew we could not make the bees leave, but we *did* know that bees always go home at dusk, so we got into the car and drove away to Lancaster. We went sightseeing, ate burgers, and came home *after* dark.

That night we made elderberry jelly, sealed the jars, washed them off, and put them on the jelly shelf. Then we scrubbed everything in the kitchen that was the least bit sweet or sticky or fruity. The bees never came back to the kitchen.

The poor bees. Maybe we will find some bees in May.

Goats and More Goats

It is the season of firsts, the first dandelion, the first robin, the first baby goats.

The first baby goats, or kids, of the season were born last night. Their very responsible mother, Buttercup, had two lovely kids, and this morning both of them were busily nursing from their mother's big, milk-filled udder.

We had been expecting the birth. Both Buttercup and Nanny went off to the billy goat last fall. Billy goats, or male goats, have a strong smell, and strong, pushy dispositions. We do not keep a billy goat for these reasons, so our goats go to another farm to be bred. When we pick them up to bring them home, our goats smell appalling! Now, five months later, Buttercup has produced fine healthy twins, and Nanny looks as if her kids will be born any minute. Both goats have been huge and clumsy for a while now.

Goat kids grow very fast. They stand up soon after they

are born and are running around before the day is over. They are lively, smart, and wonderfully entertaining.

Last season's kids kept getting out of the pasture, and we couldn't understand how they did it. They could not get under the fence, and they could not jump over it. Then one day we saw them get out and discovered their trick. The sheep have thick wool in early spring. They rub along the fence to scratch themselves. The clever little kids would jump onto a sheep's back, recover their balance, then jump again, out and over the fence.

Goat kids are weaned when they are about eight weeks old. As soon as they no longer need their mothers, we sell them. The sale of the kids pays for the goat mothers' grain for a year. From the two nanny goats we usually get four kids each year.

Once the kids are gone, we milk the two mother goats twice a day. Goats give milk from the time they freshen, or have kids, until they dry up, about nine months later.

The goats hop up onto the milking stand and eat their ration of grain, while we milk. Nanny first, Buttercup second is the order of things. Nanny is pushy and insists on being first in all things. Goats like a good, steady routine and are wonderfully cooperative if the goat owner is calm and firm with them.

We have had lots of goats. We got them to help clear away the brush when we first moved here. There was one, Blossom, who could jump any fence in a single bound. She jumped right over a Volkswagen once. We also had Coco, who was very cute, but the other goats did not like her and fought with her so often that we could not keep her.

Nanny and Buttercup are enough goats for now. They each produce about a gallon of milk a day, more than we can use, and they continue to clear away brush, wrapping their velvety pink mouths around the worst-looking thorny stems and chewing up cat briars with relish. These two goats are dear friends, milk machines, and brush cutters. Few friends could do more.

The timing of kids and weather was good this year. The kids have had a week of warm, sunny weather in which to eat, romp, and gather strength to withstand the cold spring nights.

Inside the barn cellar we have shifted the barricades around. Now the goat department is all one large space, except for the creep. The creep is an area that has a high strong fence around it to keep the adult goats out, but the fence is raised just a little so the kids can creep in. The sun shines through the open barn door and warms the creep. We put in a little hay and grain, and the tiny goats rest there and nibble at their food.

The barnyard is the kids' playpen. The curious kids explore, test, and taste everything. The barnyard was enclosed with wire fencing last fall. Then we began collecting dead cedar trees to make a picket fence outside of the wire one. Finally, about a week before the kids were due, we began to nail up pickets.

When the goats were about two days old they discovered they could slip through the wire but not through the pickets. Yesterday we finished splitting the remainder of the cedars, and we nailed up the last of the pickets. Then we chased Buttercup's pretty twins out of the doghouse where they were playing and put them back into the barnyard where we hope they will stay!

The Long Garden

Spread across the south face of a ridge, our whole farm is on a slope. In some places the hillside is very steep, but there are also broad, gentle slopes. The farmyard is one of these little plains.

The driveway crosses the hill at the base of a steep slope. Supported by a huge bank, it passes the house at roof level. The driveway bank and a series of terraces and stone walls below it is the site of my long garden. From the level of the lawn, looking uphill, there are flowers in layers. The slope holds everything up like an easel.

This garden is a living catalog of the plants we sell. The different levels of the garden provide different growing conditions. I have hot, dry banks for herbs, stony, well-drained terraces for rock garden plants, deep, rich soil and full sunshine for a flower border, shade for woodlanders, and wet ground for waterside plants. In these garden terraces I try different combinations and locations, switching plants around until I get the desired effect.

In early spring I am very busy in the long flower garden. "Little Miss Muffet," a shasta daisy, will bloom nicely only if I dig up the old plant, split the root, and replant a vigorous young piece. The nepeta has overwhelmed the peach-colored day lilies, which must be moved away. I should plant a ground cover on the bank behind the old-fashioned rose because it is hellish to weed around its thorny stems. I had better pull the foxglove seedlings out of the silvery veronica or it will be smothered.

Each little task leads to another, and each garden moment is filled with the sight and scent of flowers from earliest spring until November.

Sally Fish

Before we moved to the farm we made a firm rule not to bring home any animal unless we had a place to keep it. No goats without a fence. No dog without a doghouse. No rabbit without a cage.

The first time the rule was broken we got a goldfish. We won her at the town fair. She was in a plastic bag with some water and a knot at the top. We were excited to have won the fish and carried her happily around the fair and then home. The fish spent the night in a big blue mixing bowl.

The next day some city friends visited us. They admired the goldfish and they owned a fish bowl, so we sent the fish home with them. In her plastic bag traveling arrangement, the fish named Sally left.

By now we had lots of animals here to keep us busy and entertained, and we did not give Sally another thought. Winter came and cold weather. Our city friends, who visit often in the summer, were not seen for months.

In the spring when they returned to the farm, they brought Sally goldfish. She was growing too big for their fish bowl. They thought she would be happier in the country. They thought a rain barrel might be just the place for a growing fish to spend the summer. And they were right! Sally fish swam round and round, up and down, in the big wooden rain barrel at the corner of the porch.

We have a rain barrel at each corner of the house and around the smaller buildings, too. Rain rolls off the roofs into gutters, then down a downspout into a barrel. Beside each barrel is a watering can. I dip a watering can into a rain barrel whenever I notice some tiny plant looking dry.

These handy rain barrels all had lids to keep insects and dirt out, but none of the lids kept all the mosquitos out, and one mosquito can lay thousands of eggs! Mosquito eggs hatch in water, live there for a while as mosquito wigglers, then change into regular mosquitos and bite.

We tried wooden lids and screen lids, but until Sally goldfish the barrels were buggy.

When we dumped Sally fish into her new rain barrel home, we left the lid off so we could see her. She would also have light, and some insects could get in the water for her to eat.

The water in Sally's barrel stayed quite clear. There were no mosquitos in a buzzy cloud. Sally fish ate anything that jumped, flew, or fell into her barrel.

By the end of the summer we had learned how to keep rain barrels insect free, and we had discovered how very large a twenty-nine cent goldfish can grow to be in a large home with plenty of bugs to eat. When we looked into the greeny depths of the barrel, there was Sally swimming round and round getting bigger every day.

When the weather began to get cold and a little ice formed around the top of the barrel, we bought a ten-gallon tank and moved Sally to the attic bedroom for the winter. Goldfish can survive the winter in a pond outside; they move to the bottom and live under the ice. But rain barrels sometimes freeze solid, and even a tough old fish like Sally could not stand spending the winter in a huge ice cube.

Next spring I think we will put one fish in each rain barrel. Next summer I bet we will not have many mosquitos.

Stone End Barn

Our big stone-end barn with its wide wood overhang is about one hundred yards to the east of the house. The men who built it signed their work. They wrote their names in a large ornate hand on mud plaster on the inside of the top level of the barn. They had good reason to be proud of their work. The barn is as handsome and serviceable now as when it was built in 1816.

The barn is forty-five feet high at the peak of the roof, and the huge cornerstones, or coins, that form the corners were quarried here at the farm. Each coin was cut and dressed, or shaped, from granite boulders. These massive stones are beautifully fitted together. The corners stand straight and tall. The rest of the walls are made of large and small stones pieced together like a beautiful mosiac, each with a flat surface facing out toward the weather. The quality of the workmanship is the key to the barn's long life and excellent condition. It sheds water and so has not been affected by freezing and thawing, which destroys many old stone buildings.

The barn cellar, where the animals live in winter, has five wooden doors set in deep stone doorways that face south into the barnyard. Each doorway has a massive doorstep and a stone lintel. There are also several windows framed in thick oak planks with horizontal bars set in the frames.

The top of the barn, a huge space about fifty feet long, thirty feet deep, and very high, is divided into three bays, or sections, by the interior framing. The framing is of huge, rough-hewn timbers held together with wooden pegs. At the joints of these framing timbers, Roman numerals have been chopped with an ax. These numbers identified the pieces for the builders when they assembled the frame.

The barn builders, or mechanics, probably worked on this barn for several years. They quarried and shaped the stones, then built the stone walls. At the same time, they selected trees for the timbers. These were cut, brought to the barnsite, and squared off. Then the ends were shaped, the fit tested, and the beams marked. When the stone walls were ready for the framing, a party of local men was assembled for the day. The framework was hoisted, snugged into place, and pegged together. The barn-raising crew probably put the roof on that same day, or at least the roof framing, if not all of the shingles.

Because the barn was built on a bank, the top floor of the barn is level with the driveway. Two huge wooden

doors swing out to open the entire center bay. Wooden partitions, about eight feet high, separate the center section from haymows on either side.

We only use one haymow for hay. We carefully stack several hundred bales of hay in the big space. At first the hay is carried in through a doorway in the partition; but, as the space is filled, hay is put in over the top. If we kept more animals and more hay, we would put in hay scaffolding—poles laid between brackets built into the walls and the barn frame to stabilize the mountain of hay.

The second haymow is our general storage area. Over the extra chairs and old bicycles, we hang flowers and herbs to dry on the old scaffolding and on the tobacco rails high in the overhead space. I have two big worktables in this haymow where I make dried flower wreaths, and fresh green wreaths for Christmas. It is an ideal work space, dry and out of the wind.

The center bay of the barn is Patrick's workshop, with long workbenches and storage for tools and spare parts. We have had heavy-duty electric wiring installed for tools and lights. High above the workshop, stacked in racks supported by the barn framing, is a pile of lumber. Walnut, oak, and cherry, milled from trees here on the farm, is drying and aging. Someday we may use this wood for a special project.

Baby Bunnies

One of our pet rabbits escaped from her cage a few weeks ago. She knew where the food and shelter were so she stayed in the barn and barnyard, but she eluded us when we tried to catch her. We were pretty sure she was expecting babies soon, so we were especially anxious to put her back into her safe, warm home.

One afternoon Pierre and I went into the barn to see Nanny's beautiful new little goat daughter, and there on the barn floor in a nest of hay were two tan-and-white bunnies. They were fully covered with fur, and their tiny ears lay back flat against their little curled-up backs.

I fixed a nest box in a big rabbit cage just outside the barn and stuffed the cage and nest box with plenty of sweet hay. I put in rabbit food, water, some carrot ends, and a cabbage leaf. Then I sat down about three feet from the baby bunnies to wait.

The mama rabbit came and looked at me and the bunnies. She let me pick her up and put her in the cage. I went back and got the two bunnies and put them in with her. The mama rabbit pushed her babies into the nest box, and began eating the food I had placed in the cage for her. Once, a baby bunny, loose in the barnyard, lost nearly half of its ear when a chicken pecked it. Cages are for protection as much as confinement.

The mama rabbit has pulled out a lot of her own undercoat and covered the sleeping bunnies with this light, soft fluff. We can see the bunnies tumbling around in the nest box, but they have not come out since the move. Mother and children are doing fine.

When the rabbits are not escaping, they live in a wire apartment house in the barnyard. Each rabbit has a cage of its own to prevent fighting and breeding.

Patrick's daughter, Marie, who lives in town with her mother and visits us on weekends and holidays, acquired the first rabbit. Rabbit manure is very welcome in the nursery which almost justifies keeping rabbits. Our children are so awful about it that we can't eat the rabbits, and the rabbits are so awful that they just make more.

Busy Days

The morning rush is over, the sun is high in the sky, and my list of things to be done today is waiting for attention.

April and May are the busiest months here. We dig, pack, and ship hundreds of little plants each Monday and Tuesday in the spring. Garden designers and landscape contractors ordered the plants during the winter, asking for delivery at spring planting time. We mark the dates on the calendar; then we ship the growing plants, packed in styrofoam noodles, for arrival at the requested planting date. Plants are shipped by bus or United Parcel Service over a five state area, arriving the same day or the next day.

We have all had breakfast, all the farm animals have been fed, Pierre is off to school, nine boxes of plants have been delivered to the shipper, two boxes of cut flowers have been put on the bus for Philadelphia, several hundred pots of plants for a community garden project have been watered, and a restaurant order of watercress and lettuce is washed, sorted, and packed, waiting in the cool springhouse for pick-up by the chef. After a coffee and a sit-down, I will begin to dig and cut, gather and pack today's harvest, keeping a careful eye on my list.

The grass needs mowing, some nursery patches need weeding, and many pots of seedlings need transplanting. A florist will come today to chose the flowers for a wedding she is doing next weekend. A local landscaper plans to stop by and look at suitable perennials for a dry, sunny bank.

The chef just picked up his darling little lettuces. He was very pleased. This is a new lettuce for us, 'Tom Thumb,' sweet little heads about the size of tennis balls. We have hundreds and hundreds of them, some half-inch high seedlings for next month, some that will be ready tomorrow or next week.

Each crop—lettuce for a restaurant kitchen, cut flowers for a florist, herbs and perennials for the landscaper—requires time, care, attention, and luck. If the weather gets hot, the lettuce will bolt, turning bitter. If there is a violent rainstorm, flower petals are damaged and the florist cannot use them. If garden fashions change, as they do from season to season, hundreds of plants of a certain variety will go unsold.

Farming, any sort of farming, is not for the faint-hearted. There are so many things beyond control that can go wrong, and do go wrong. Farmers get in the habit of being thrilled by small successes and shrugging off small failures. With farming there is always next year. Next year the weather may be better, the timing will be better, marketing plans will be better.

The weather has been gentle this spring. We have all worked terribly hard and we have been lucky, too. We are lucky to have a pair of humming birds nesting in the big old pine tree within sight of the house. We noticed them when they first arrived. They buzzed around the tree and drove away a pair of nesting mourning doves. They dive-bomb any other birds trying to move into their exclusive piece of real estate. Now, from the attic window, with binoculars we can look into their tiny nest and see two newly-hatched hummingbirds!

This afternoon when I am finished with my things-to-do list, I am going to move some red flowers into the long flower border for the hummingbirds. Humingbirds like tube-shaped blossoms, especially pink, red, and orange ones. I hope to keep them happily feeding within sight of the porch. Hummingbirds don't pay the bills, but our life is richer for them.

The Cats' Cooperative Day Care Center

Our cats never touch poultry. Our first kittens were raised in the chicken yard with a few large hens that outweighed them by pounds. The cats and chickens reached an easy peace very soon. No chicken or chick, duck or duckling, is chased, frightened, or eaten by a cat. It simply is not done, and the cats are smart enough to know it. The payoff for the cats is that chicken feed attracts rats and mice, which cats do chase, frighten, and eat.

There are four lady cats presently living in our barn. They are closely related—mother, daughters, sisters, and aunts—and they keep the cats' co-operative day care center.

Kitty Marie walked into our lives as a very small kitten with bright blue eyes and a stiff tail carried straight up behind herself. She is a gray-and-black striped tabby cat with four white feet. About a year later she had a daughter, Pochinko. Pochinko has long black fur and a white face. Next came Calico, a white cat with big spots of orange and black. The last to arrive was Ghostly, who is all white except for a black tail and one black ear.

This troop of lovelies lives in the barn, catching mice and lapping fresh goat milk. They are barn cats, not tame pet cats. They never come into our house, and they rarely allow themselves to be picked up or petted. And we try not to interfere with their cattish existence.

In the spring we know that kittens are due when the cat mothers are too fat to slip through some of their favorite tiny places. We know that kittens have been born when a newly thin, tired-looking cat comes into the barn, or when one of the cats does not appear at milking time.

Kitty Marie had Pochinko on her own; but the next year, when both cats had kittens, Kitty Marie helped Pochinko clean, feed, and care for her kittens. Kitty Marie's tiny newborn kitties, blind and helpless, shared a nest with three-week old kittens, open-eyed and playful. Both cat mothers took turns feeding, washing, and caring for the whole lot.

Later in the summer several kittens disappeared and we gave one away. Calico stayed.

The next spring all three cat mothers had kittens and again they took turns with the responsibilities of motherhood. If Pochinko was sunning herself and Kitty Marie was hunting, Calico could be found with the kittens—her own and those of the other mothers. Again, by fall some kittens had vanished and some went to new homes. Ghostly stayed to join the barn cats here.

This spring we were passing the barnyard and happened upon Ghostly having her first kitten. Pochinko picked up the tiny newborn kitten and carried it into the barn. Ghostly followed and gave birth to two more kittens as Pochinko cleaned off the first born. Last night I saw Ghostly nursing one tiny kitten (her own), one very large kitten (Kitty Marie's), and two others (probably Pochinko's).

The cat population is carefully controlled by the cats themselves, who seem to know how many cats are enough. A very large black-and-white tomcat lives at a neighboring farm and is undoubtedly the father. He probably has something to do with the vanishing kittens. No young male cat has survived his first summer here, and no tomcat lives in our barn.

There is one very cute kitten, black with a white tail. I wonder if it will be here in the fall. I wonder about the vanishing kittens, too, but I am glad they disappear or we would have a cat army.

Fences First

Our first farm animals were sheep and before the sheep came the fence. We cleared a fence line, cut locust and cedar posts, and hired a post hole digger. The man with his tractor-mounted machine put the posts in quickly and firmly. We bought enough wire to fence two acres and a large box of fence staples to nail the fence to the posts. But when the fence wire was delivered, the rolls were too heavy to move and we had no idea how to get the fence up. We called around and found a couple of farm boys to help us.

The boys rolled one of the heavy rolls of wire to a corner post and attached the end of the wire to the post. Then they unrolled the wire along the fence line. Next they made a fence puller from a pair of two-by-fours, drilling holes through both pieces of lumber and fitting the holes with nuts and bolts. The loose end of the unrolled wire was sandwiched between the two boards.

They wrapped a chain around the fence puller and hooked the other end of the chain to their tractor and pulled. The fence wire snapped up tight against the fence posts and was nailed into place with fence staples. The two boys got the fence up in about two hours and taught us how to do it ourselves.

Patrick made gates—two small gates to walk through and one large one to accommodate a truck or tractor. When the gates were hung and hooked we got our sheep, John Dear and Lily, a pair of Southdowns.

We planned on Lily producing daughters and our flock enlarging itself. The first spring Lily had two little ram lambs. She was a wonderful mother; the lambs prospered and grew.

We were careful not to name them or treat them as pets, and they were sent off to return as lamb chops.

Lily has produced twin ram lambs each year for four years. We have enjoyed excellent lamb and we are not complaining, but our flock has not grown. John Dear got to be very large and rammy. He is now living at someone else's farm with many ewes, and we transport Lily to him. We still dream of a grassy hillside dotted with sheep.

In June, after school is out, we call for the sheepshearer. We lure Lily up from the pasture to the barnyard and, after a tiny sheep rodeo, Mr. Stoltzfus, the shearer, sits her up on her tail, with her legs in the air, and gives her a haircut. His big electric clipper slides neatly and safely across her skin, shearing her wool. In a couple of minutes, Lily is ten or twelve pounds lighter and an entirely different shape. After her feet are trimmed, we send her back to the pasture, where the goats don't recognize her.

Mr. Stoltzfus rolls the wool into a bundle and ties it with paper twine. He will take Lily's fleece, together with the wool from his own sheep, to a hat factory. There, the wool is cleaned and processed, and made into wool felt hats.

Lily is back out in the pasture now, head down chewing, growing a new fleece. The bell on her collar is ringing her contentment.

June Weeds

It is June. Every tree is in full leaf now. The pale tints of spring are gone, and the woods are dark with green light. In the open sunshine the grass in the pastures is thick and lush. The flower gardens and nursery beds are bright, dappled sheets of color. The air is velvety smooth and perfume-laden, almost edible.

In April and May, as we rush along planting and digging

and selling plants, we think we are keeping up with the explosion of growth going on all around us. By the first of June, we know we are beaten again. The jump-up June weeds, big and juicy, have captured all the steep banks and rough places that have not been mowed, grazed, or cultivated.

We have gotten to know the weeds very well. We know about their roots, their flowers (for they all do have flowers), and their season of going to seed. We hoe or pull out tons of weeds each season. It is extremely trying to deal with this green tide, but the saving grace of weeds is that this year's crop of weeds, composted, is next year's humus. Thinking of weeds as a resource and realizing that pulling them is accomplishing two things at once is a boon to weeders.

I know a great many weeds intimately after years of weeding. There are the fleshy, fast-growing annual weeds that seem to pop up by the millions after each rain. These are easily pulled. Their water-filled stems and the bits of soil attached to their roots help speed decomposition. The trick with annual weeds is to pull them and compost them before they go to seed. If you do this consistently, they will cease to be a problem.

Perennial weeds, the ones that have more or less permanent root systems, are another story. They are hard or impossible to pull. A hefty yank gets the weeder a handful of top, but the root of the problem is not much disturbed. The roots have to be dug out of the ground. Most perennial weeds will sprout over and over from bits of root left behind. This devilish group of plants will also prosper and grow on an ordinary compost heap.

We compost perennial weeds in a different area from our regular compost pile. This means that the weeder needs two baskets or two wheelbarrows, sorting the vegetable trash as he goes along.

Problem weeds are piled in even layers that are either covered with fresh chicken manure or sprinkled with a large amount of nitrogen fertilizer. The plants then grow themselves to death.

So we weed and weed, pushing one barrow of weeds to one compost pile and the other barrow to the other. I hope to live here long enough to see most of the weeds become flowers. This happens in old gardens where weeds have been pulled for many years and the dormant weed seeds in the soil have finally been depleted.

The weeds are replaced by poppies, johnny jump-ups, primroses, and blue phlox. Poppies and johnny jump-ups must have gotten their names from their habit of appearing, unplanted, in the oddest places.

Picnics and Ice Cream

Tomorrow is Pierre's last day of school. The end of school is the beginning of our summer, even though the calendar shows summer to be several weeks away.

Pierre chose lunch-making as his chore last summer. I hope he will do it again. I loved having a noon surprise delivered to me in a basket.

Pierre's only criterion for lunch is cold food. He filled the lunch basket from kitchen and garden with a child's perception of a perfect meal. The choices and combinations were funny but often delicious: cheese and apple sandwich (slices of cheese on both sides of a thick piece of apple, no bread); lettuce, peanut butter, and pepperoni on rye; raw green peas direct from the garden and nothing else. Many days lunch was a melon for each of us, no sharing! A more ambitious lunch was a melon basket filled with chunks of cantelope, blueberries, and raspberries decorated with flowers. Once lunch was an

JANE REED LENNON

unopened can of sardines that Pierre dropped off as he ran by, too busy with kid stuff to "cook."

I'm too busy with garden stuff to cook much, either. We like summer meals of salads, fruit, bread, and cheese. We have a little grill outside where we cook chicken or burgers in the twilight. A real culinary thrill for summer is ice cream. We have a small ice cream freezer, the hand-crank kind. Fresh fruit, goat's milk, and an egg or two are churned into a delicious treat.

A visitor once suggested that it was tedious to crank ice cream. We decided to make some, and he proved to himself that he was wrong. We filled the churn with the ingredients, filled the outside bucket with cracked ice and salt, and started to turn. The visitor wanted to feel the cream harden as he cranked so the assorted children present had to badger him for a turn at the crank. Soon the freezer bucket was coated with frost, and the ice cream in the churn got stiffer and stiffer. The children ran inside for bowls and spoons. In about half an hour, start to finish, we all sat down to an ice cream treat.

I put some plastic cartons of water in the freezer today. We'll have plenty of ice to make ice cream tomorrow. After all, school will be out, it must be summer.

Ah, June!

The Wren Family

When we took down the storm windows that enclose our porch in winter, a wren fussed and chattered at us. Before all the windows were hauled to the barn, the tiny, noisy bird had moved into a bird's-nest gourd hanging from a porch rafter. We had planned to hang the gourd in a tree, but the wrens couldn't wait.

During the next weeks, two wrens busily carried twigs and bits of grass into the gourd. We heard scratching noises from inside the wren's house, and we watched the gourd swing and bump around as the two tiny birds arranged their nest.

At first, when the birds began building, they would not go into the hole in the gourd if we were looking directly at them. They waited, perched on a basket hanging from a rafter, until we looked away, then they darted into their home.

As the days went by, the wrens became bolder, or

perhaps more rushed, and they ignored us—except to chatter and scold from inside the gourd.

In pleasant weather we eat our meals on the porch, right under the bird's-nest gourd, so we had a daily view at very close quarters of our wren neighbors. While the eggs were incubating, the wrens were calm and quiet. When the baby birds hatched, the noise and activity increased enormously!

As the baby birds grew, one adult wren stood guard, baby-sitting, just inside the hole, and the other hunted and carried food constantly. Pierre and I clocked them—one trip every three minutes. An adult bird would fly from the perch on the gourd, grab a grasshopper nymph, a tiny green caterpillar, or another little bug from the lawn or garden, and return to the perch. The hunter would pass the morsel of food to its mate and fly off again, while the mate stuffed the bugfood into one of the tiny open mouths.

We hoped to see the baby birds leave the nest, but the clever wrens launched their brood when we were away from the porch. We knew they were gone one morning when the nest gourd was quiet and still.

A few days later we saw the adults, or maybe another pair of wrens, rearranging the nest inside the gourd, and the process started again.

There are hundreds or thousands of birds around the farmyard and gardens, and there are millions or billions of insects in the same area. One delectable thing about having a flower farm is that the flowers attract many butterflies.

For every butterfly, there was once an extremely hungry caterpillar.

Last evening I went out to cut dill flowers for one of my favorite customers—the chef. I found many bare stalks in the dill patch. The feathery leaves and flower heads were gone. Eaten, but by whom? I looked among the remaining dill plants and found some chartreuse-and-black striped caterpillars, two inches long and the thickness of a pencil.

Once upon a time I would have squashed them, but I've learned that these greedy guys will transform themselves into monarch butterflies. With Pierre's help, I picked up all the caterpillars among the dill. Then we checked the parsley, fennel, and chervil patches and collected more of the villains.

Pierre carried them out to the pasture and unloaded them carefully among the wildflowers and grasses there. We are not nearly so kind or considerate about all caterpillars, but we have come to recognize many, and we relocate the ones that give us pleasure as butterflies.

Our Eighteenth-Century Farmhouse

Some friends asked us to spend a camping holiday with them. We declined. We have been camping ever since we moved here. Patrick calls this house our stone tent.

Luckily we moved to the farm in the summer. The old house seemed like a vacation cottage that lacked some of the conveniences of modern living but made up for it by being charming and novel.

We are connected to the outside world by a very long driveway under which are telephone and electric wires, so we are plugged in. But, other than the electricity and phone hookups, time has stood still for these buildings. Nothing has been added, changed, or covered over.

The masonry walls are sturdy and secure, but they were not laid up by the same skillful hands that built the barn. The house was built in two stages, the southern end with the springhouse first, the north end and the huge fireplace a little later. Though we don't know exactly when the house was started, it was here in its present form before 1750.

The original house included the cellar springhouse room, a first-floor room, and an attic room under the roof. The north wall was probably wood, with a lean-to shed attached. The main room was almost doubled in size to its present fifteen by twenty-four feet when the addition with the huge fireplace and chimney was built. At that time the roof was raised to create another second-floor room with an attic above it.

The stone walls of the house are more than two feet thick. The windows, with their tiny panes, are set in deep windowsills. The window frames are made of logs, squared only on the side that faces the sash, and pegged together.

The flooring on the first level is not original, but the hand-cut beams and floorboards for the second floor and the attic are very, very old. The marks of the saw on these boards show they were hand-sawn before the advent of circular saws.

This house was built by German Swiss settlers who came to the area at the beginning of the eighteenth century. The construction of the roof and the shape of the huge chimney, built *inside* the house, are clues to the builders. We think that, if they could come back, they would still feel very much at home here almost two hundred and fifty years later.

A long, narrow porch faces east and south across the front of the house. It is the heart of our farm. In the summer we live on the porch—cooking, eating, planning, and working there. The porch is warmed by the morning sun and shaded by the house against the heat of a summer afternoon. After supper we sit there in the twilight. White flowers glow in the long garden. Fireflies rise from the lawn into the summer night. From the pasture we hear the soft banging of sheep and goat bells.

My parents gave us a new outhouse when we moved here. They had a local carpenter build and deliver it, complete with little moon-shaped cutouts on either side. The outhouse is carefully located downhill and away from our spring. It is close enough, but not too close, to the house and is tucked in under a huge old lilac bush.

The house does have water—a pitcher pump mounted on the drainboard of a small sink in the corner of the main room. A pipe connects the pump to the spring in the cellar below. One stroke of the handle yields about eight ounces of fresh, cold spring water. The sink has a drain that carries excess water out into the meadow to the west of the house. The supply pipe to the pump and the drainpipe are the total plumbing of the house. We never require a plumber's services.

Bathing is a bit complicated. For summer we have an outdoor shower with solar-heated water. We pump a bucket or two of water, pour it into a black-painted tank, and let the sun warm the water. The floor of the shower area is paved with stones, and when it is not being used as a shower, it is a small terrace adjacent to the herb garden.

In winter our wood stove warms quantities of water. We pump water into buckets and pour it into a tank

attached to the stove. The hot-water tank has a spigot, and
we have a big, old-fashioned tin tub that we use for
bathing in front of the fire. The only real inconvenience is
that the used bath water must be carried outside since
there is no drain.

The kitchen could be in our living room, but I would rather be inconvenienced than have cooking smells all through the house, so we use the summer kitchen year round. The summer kitchen is the enclosed north end of the porch. It has a gas stove, a refrigerator, some small counters, and cupboards. There are nails driven into the rafters to hang all the pots, pans, kitchen implements, baskets, and other kitchen necessities. The summer kitchen is about eight feet square and, like the galley of a boat, is wonderfully efficient if everything is kept in its proper place.

Some day we will add to the house, but we will do it very carefully. We are living in a house that is an historic treasure, and we feel a great responsibility to both past and future generations. For now, we live in our dear stone tent in much the same way as people have lived here for hundreds of years.

Chicken for Dinner

We have just finished dinner. Everything we ate, except the bread in the stuffing, was grown here on the farm. The menu was roast chicken with herb and onion stuffing; lettuce, watercress, and hardboiled egg salad; and peaches for dessert.

We don't grow all of our food, or try to, but we do grow special treats like snow peas, interesting salad greens, chickens, and ducks—foods that can be grown easily along with our other garden and barnyard chores.

The chickens and ducks we grow for meat are ordered from a hatchery. On the day the chicks or ducks hatch, they are popped into a special cardboard box and sent to us in the mail. They must be sent as soon as they come out of their shells because they will not eat or drink during their trip in the mail. Each new chick has a two-day food supply inside its tiny body when it hatches and will eat its first meal when it is three days old.

The post office telephones when the chicks arrive because our mailman has a long route and does not get to us until late afternoon. To save the chicks from this long journey, we drive to town and pick them up.

The newly hatched chicks or ducklings must be kept warm and protected. They are very delicate and almost brainless—a bad combination! They need food, clean water, and dry ground on which to stand.

In a few weeks they are big enough to be moved to a little outdoor yard with a secure fence and an A-frame shelter to protect them from rain. The fence is more to keep larger animals out than to keep chicks in. They are easy prey for foxes, weasels, and skunks, all of which consider young chicks a special treat.

We feed the chicks and ducklings large quantities of specially mixed grains and supply them with fresh water. When they are about six weeks old, they have outgrown their baby pen and are moved to a larger yard of the same kind. Here they scratch and peck around for salad and insects in the grassy yard and continue eating the grain we put out for them. The table is always set in the chicken yard. The chickens continue to grow at a great rate. They are roasting chickens specially bred to grow quickly to a large meaty size. Most are fully grown in less than sixteen weeks. Growing from a two-ounce chick to a ten-pound chicken in four months represents a lot of eating and a good diet.

We care for them, worry about them, and protect them as long as they are growing. When they are the right size,

we harvest them, like any other carefully grown crop. Poultry is sent off to the butcher, and returned to the farm as neatly packaged meat.

It is wonderful to sit down to a fine, big meal and say, "I grew this food."

Swings

The day Patrick hung our swings I got a lump in my throat. I remembered my own dad taking a big coil of rope out of his car and asking my brother and sisters to guess why he had brought it home.

I remember carrying a brace-and-bit drill and big eyebolts to the woods. My brother and sister carried the ladder, Dad carried the rope, and my mother carried some boards. My grandfather carried along a chair in which to sit and supervise. Very quickly we had two swings, with board seats and a knotted climbing rope, in the huge hickory tree at the edge of the woods.

About thirty years later a similar parade of enthusiasts achieved the same results in a walnut tree and an ash tree for another child. This time Pierre danced around excitedly as the ladder was placed against a huge branch, holes were drilled, bolts set, and ropes attached. Patrick put two swings in one tree and a tire swing on a knotted climbing rope in the second tree.

The swings were attached to eyebolts because tying ropes around a tree branch usually kills the branch. The back and forth of swinging quickly wears away the bark, and the part of the branch beyond the swing starves, dies, and eventually falls.

When I am enjoying a ride on one of our swings with my feet reaching out toward the treetops, I like to think of a delighted cave person on a vine swing thousands of years ago swinging back and forth just for the joy of it. I like the bounce of the branch, the rush of air going by, and the power of my legs reaching out and pulling back, sending the swing higher and higher.

> *How do you like to go up in a swing*
> *Up in the air so blue?*
> *Oh, I do think it the pleasantest thing*
> *Ever a child can do!*

Robert Louis Stevenson obviously felt just as I do about swings.

Tools

Sometimes I think about the stunning amount of work required to keep this farm functioning. And almost every time I think that, I also think how fortunate I am. I am doing what I like to do. I love to mow the grass. The end result is so pleasing! The sweet green smell and the velvet tidyness of a newly mowed lawn are summer treats.

I used to hate the job. The mower wouldn't start or, if it did, the noise would drive me crazy. One day I complained about lawn mowers and mowing to a visiting friend. The friend offered to check out our mowers and explain their various parts and foibles to me. He also suggested earplugs to reduce the noise.

What a difference! Now I keep the mowers in good working order, servicing them between each use. I change the oil, clean the filters, sharpen the blades, and do minor repairs before major problems occur. I'm no longer at the mercy of a balky mower or the repairman's schedule.

When I'm ready to mow, I check the oil, fill the gas tank, put in my earplugs, and pull the starter. Off I go!

I used to hate the mowers, but it wasn't the mowers, the problem was me. If the mower ran at all, I used it very hard and thoughtlessly. The machine got no thanks from me and no maintenance. It was a battle. Now it's a working relationship.

Is it funny to think of having relationships with tools? I think relationship is the right word. Finding the correct tool for the job, the correct tool for the user, and using that tool properly must all come before getting on with the job. I know that a tree *can* be planted with a butter knife if one is determined enough, but how futile to waste so much time and effort!

Now when I buy a new tool I try it on. I hold it in my hands to make sure it fits them. If I will be using the tool wearing work gloves, I try it with work gloves. I lift the tool to feel its weight and balance. I go through all the motions of using the tool.

I have tried shovels and rakes with handles too thick for me to hold comfortably. I have sampled fine-looking hedge trimmers that caused the knuckles of my left hand to bash against the knuckles of my right hand when I snipped an imaginary hedge. I guess the designer of that tool forgot that hands would be necessary to hold his neat-looking tool.

Hand clippers, which I use many hours each week, are especially important to me. Once, on the assumption that more expensive was better, I ordered an extremely fancy

pair. The wretched things arrived and were very heavy—so heavy, in fact, that they are still in our tool building, years later, almost never used.

A tool is an extension of the hand, or arm, or person that uses it. If it is the right tool for the worker and the right tool for the job, the work is easy and enjoyable.

When I begin a job, if it seems a struggle, I stop for a minute and consider the tool. Then I usually walk back to the toolshed and try something else, or a combination of tools.

We have very stony ground here. When it is soft and moist, the small stones are pushed aside by the blade of a shovel. If the ground is dry and hard, the shovel bounces off those same stones. Back to the tool building for a grub hoe. The grub hoe is heavier, and its own weight carries it down among the stones. If the grub hoe won't do the job, next in line is a pick. The pick is pointed and heavy. It buries itself among the stones and loosens them. But if the pick cannot handle the work, there is still the digging bar. It is very heavy, sixty pounds, and its narrow, wedge-shaped end can get down beside a rock while its length becomes a lever to pry the offending rock from its place in the ground. There is pleasure in meeting the challange of digging the impossible hole.

We used to admire some of the huge rocks in our woods, saying that when we had a bulldozer come to do other work, we would have the dozer man move a few of them out of the woods and closer to the house where we could enjoy seeing them. It never happened. But, in the meantime, we have acquired many tools and learned how to use them; and we have collected quite a few of those huge immovable rocks and put them where we want them by ourselves.

There were no bulldozers at Stonehenge and no superhumans. There were rollers and ropes and levers and determined people—the right tools in the right hands.

Thunderstorm

A big thunderstorm blew in just at twilight. The western sky, the last to darken on summer evenings, was suddenly as purple-black as a bruise. The wind picked up and blew the tree leaves, exposing their silvery undersides.

Sandy dog took her thunderstorm position inside the house, and I rushed around picking up tools and doing a mental checklist: Car windows closed? Lawn mowers put away? Laundry off the clothes line?

The rain arrived with a huge crash of thunder. I sat on the porch in the storm dark and watched and listened and felt the storm all around me. While the storm was overhead I could not see the lightning, but the waves and rolls and booms of thunder shook the porch floor under my feet. Buckets of water rushed off the roof and bubbled into the rainbarrels.

The storm continued eastward. I sat and watched it travel for the next hour. The flashes and crashes in the distant sky were wonderful. Clouds and trees were momentarily backlighted by the lightning. The beautiful big pine tree on the lawn was silhouetted by great white flashes in the dark sky. The thunderstorm sound-and-light show was a real ripsnorter, and the porch provided a ringside seat.

One last distant flash of lightning showed Lucky Duck happily dabbling in a puddle and my workbasket soggy on the lawn.

Gypsy Moths

In July, gypsy moths lay their eggs in masses covered with a fuzzy tan substance that weatherproofs the eggs and protects them from egg-eating birds. The egg masses are laid on walls, on trees, on buildings, under cars, and in any other sheltered spot. Egg masses of the gypsy moth are often carried unknowingly from one area to another by summer visitors and campers.

The following spring when the eggs hatch, the tiny worms have another means of dispersal. They climb up into the trees and eat the leaves during the night. In the morning, to hide from the birds, they lower themselves out of the trees on long silken filaments and hide on the ground. The prevailing winds spread the pesty worms through the woods by blowing them from tree to tree while they are dangling on their fine threads.

When it is worm time in the woods, there is the sound of a million mouths chewing and a steady rain of worm casts. Bright sunlight in the usually shady woods signals a serious problem.

In June the fully-grown caterpillars make flimsy cocoons from which the moths emerge a few weeks later. The white female moths usually stay where they emerge from their chrysalises, while the tan male moths flop and fly around for a few days. Then new eggs are laid, and this disgusting pest is dormant until the following spring.

Luckily gypsy moths do have natural enemies. Tiny wasps parasitize the eggs. Mice, shrews, and birds eat the caterpillars and chrysalises.

Damage to the trees, especially oak trees (the gypsy moth's favorite food in this woods) is considerable. The caterpillars eat all the leaves, which are the food factories for the trees. If the tree is strong and healthy, it produces another crop of leaves and begins to replace lost food. The second year the caterpillars repeat their voracious removal of all the leaves, and many trees no longer have enough food reserve to make another crop of leaves. The trees starve and die.

Mature trees—the huge old ones—and young, crowded trees are the most frequent victims. Vigorous middle-sized trees seem able to tough it out. It takes several years for the predator population to catch up with the gypsy moth population. The first two years (or worm seasons) are really awful. Then the moths are usually reduced to a low but steady population, and the best oaks survive.

In our area of mixed hardwood forests, three different plagues have attacked trees in the last fifty years. First came the chestnut blight, then the elm disease, and now the gypsy moth. The mixed forest survives all these because it is a mixture of many trees. It changes character with the arrival of a plague, but the whole survives and flourishes.

The caterpillars are gone. The trees will grow their leafy crowns again, and we will be able to enjoy our woods once more.

Silkies

Our delightful little pet chickens are called Silkies. They are about the size of a softball. They lay tiny eggs, and they would not make good fried chicken. They are just for decoration. The Silkies have fluffy white feathers, blue skin, blue beaks, and blue feet! And they have a spot of iridescent turquoise on each side of their head. The hens have perky white hats of feathers on the tops of their heads, and the rooster has an odd comb that looks like a big, purple raspberry.

Our Silkie rooster is rather fierce. He fights my yellow

barnyard boots. He flies at them, his legs and feet stuck out in front, hitting the boots with his spurs or toenails. It is a good thing that the boots are tough. The Silkie rooster never fights other people or other shoes, he keeps his distance and acts like a model chicken. His grudge is with my boots, I think, and not with me.

One Silkie made her nest in a corner of the barn and filled it with acorn-size eggs. When we found her with the nest, we moved her to the protection of a biddy house. The Silkie hens are good mothers, but they frequently choose a poor spot for their nests or move their newly hatched chicks to dangerous places. One hen nested in a bucket; and, although she could fly out, her chicks could not, and they starved. Another little hen moved her chicks to the woods for privacy and a fox or possum ate all of them.

The biddy house is a cage that keeps the mother hen, or biddy, confined but allows her chicks to go in and out. The chicks never stray far from their mother. There is food and water in the biddy house, and it is safe and warm for the young chicks.

A few days after they hatch, the young chicks go out and begin to explore in the barnyard. Their mother, watching from the biddy house, clucks and scolds, seeming to give them instructions. Whenever there is a noise or a flurry in the barnyard, the tiny chicks dash, screaming, for the shelter of the biddy house and their mother.

The chicks are about a month old now. They are not pretty yet because they do not have all their feathers. This morning when I fed the animals, I noticed a fuss in the biddy house. All six big chicks and the mother Silkie were inside peeping noisily. I fed the animals and left the yard; then I looked back and still the chicks were in the biddy house, complaining.

Overnight they had grown too big to fit through the openings. They had just managed to squeeze inside to get to bed last night, but they could not squeeze out this morning. I took a slat off the bottom of their house. The mother and her six half-grown Silkies are off on a tour around the garden, but they will probably return to the opened biddy house to eat and sleep.

Springhouse Cleaning

Yesterday it was so still and sultry that the leaves on the trees hung down wilted and limp. The flowers drooped, and even the insects hid from the heat. The farm animals took refuge from the glaring sunlight in the shade of trees, and the whole farm was dead quiet.

We retreated to the cellar springhouse. This little room is dug into the hillside and insulated by it. The temperature is further affected by the bubbling stream of clear water that runs out from under the back wall, crossing the floor in an open stone channel and exiting under the doorstep, where it becomes a little brook that runs across the lawn. The spring water maintains a constant temperature of about forty degrees, winter and summer.

In winter the springhouse feels warm, and in summer it is blissfully cool. With a minimum-maximum thermometer, we have recorded a variation of about thirty degrees. The coldest temperature we have recorded there was about thirty-six degrees during below-zero winter weather. The warmest was sixty-five degrees during a very hot spell in late summer when the outside temperature was hovering at one hundred.

The springhouse is the location of our household water source, and it is also our pantry. For more than two hundred years mothers on this farm have sent their children down to the springhouse to bring up a jar of jam or a basket of potatoes for dinner. We still store food there, although we have an electric refrigerator. We have long shelves for home-canned fruit, jam, and pickles, and we store potatoes in bins along the walls. The springhouse floor is hard-packed clay, smooth and shiny from generations of feet.

Yesterday Pierre and I carried a couple of lawn chairs into the springhouse and sat in natural air-conditioned comfort. Then, revived by the cool air and some minty iced tea, we gave the place a good cleaning.

We swept out the empty vegetable bins so they would be ready for this year's potato crop. We tidied the canning shelves and organized them with all the empty jars at one end, ready to be refilled. This season's jams and jellies are arranged in shining rows—strawberry jam, sour cherry preserves, wild cherry jelly, blueberry jam. Such rich bounty, lined up and waiting, ready for use on our own table or to be given as Christmas presents.

When the pantry cleaning work was done, we aimed our efforts at the water channel in the cellar floor. The spring carries sand and grit out of the hill and deposits it in the channel. What a perfect occupation for a hot day! The cold water flowing over our bare feet as we scooped out the grit kept us cool and comfortable while we worked on a job that accomplished two things at once. The channel was cleared so the water could flow more freely, and I gathered a good supply of stony grit, which I use to pot special little plants.

We were so refreshed and inspired by our watery work that we continued out the door and across the lawn, clearing the spring course to the edge of the woods. Water iris, mint, watercress, jewel weed, and other plants that thrive with wet feet were choking the small stream. We cut back some of the plants and pulled out others, working our way downhill.

Our pulling and chopping disturbed the many inhabitants of the stream. Crayfish, that look like tiny lobsters, scuttled away into the churned-up muddy water. Newts, salamanders, and red-spotted efts appeared, then slipped from sight among the loose stacked stones that line the spring bank. Frogs, big old ones and tiny young ones, plopped into the water and swam out of sight.

As we worked, the water became muddy and swirling; but as we moved downhill the silt settled, the running water swept the debris along, and upstream the water cleared, leaving shining water-washed stones.

When we finished the job, the entire run of water was visible for the first time in several months. Patches of bright blue sky were reflected in the surface, and we heard the sound of water chuckling and gurgling its way across the lawn and down the hill.

Back on the porch, we put our pruny, water-wrinkled feet up on the railing while we sat and admired our day's work. A big frog hit the water with a fat plop.

Berry Time

I have never bought blackberries or wineberries in a store. I don't think they are often sold. They are hard to pick and very delicate. When the berries are their ripest and sweetest, they leak juice on the fingers of the picker. They have to be eaten right away or perhaps saved for supper, but they won't keep much longer than that.

Wineberries ripen first. They grow in fat, slightly sticky bunches at the tips of long canes. The wineberry canes, or stems, are red with a fuzz of prickles and thorns. They grow all around the farm in the half shade. There are some quite near the house, and during wineberry season we nip out in the morning and pick a few handfuls to eat on breakfast cereal.

Blackberries ripen later, when the weather is at its hottest and stickiest. A blackberry picker has to be very determined and very fond of the fruit. Blackberry picking is not something you can decide to do when you are out for a picnic wearing sandals and shorts! The berries grow in thickets or big, tangled clumps. The long canes droop to the ground, root there, and grow up again.

Blackberry pickers wear jeans, sometimes two pairs, one on top of the other, and high boots even in August when it is ninety degrees. We go stomping and scrabbling among the thorns to collect the fat, black, juicy berries. Plonk! One berry for the bucket, then one for the picker. We pick along the old stone walls that surround the hayfield. The dark green leaves with silver, thorn-lined backs shade and protect the bunches of big, sweet fruit.

Soon our buckets are full. Sweaty and covered with red scratches and blackberry juice, we leave the bright hot sunlight of the open field for the woods and the path home. In the shade of the trees, the air is ten to fifteen degrees cooler.

Refreshed, we survey our harvest—almost two gallons of berries and three full pickers. We will have an enormous blackberry pie for supper; and later, in the cool of the evening, I'll make some blackberry jelly.

Blackberry jelly, dark purple and shiny, glitters like jewels on toast and tastes like a summer day. In good berry years there is enough rain to fill every berry with water and enough sunshine to turn the water into sweet, tasty juice.

Sometimes there is blackberry honey, too. Honeybees are very fond of blackberry juice. When the berries are ripe and plentiful the whole hive feeds them. Our beekeeping neighbor takes blackberry honey from his hives at the end of the season. The dark purple honey smells of blackberries and tastes divine.

Humans and honeybees are not the only berry fanciers. A mockingbird built its nest in a particularly choice thicket near the house, and the mocker and his family ate every berry! They flew out and complained when we approached *their* thicket, shouting and flying in our faces until we moved well away. We watched the mockingbirds from a distance as they went round the thicket, eating only ripe berries and leaving the green ones for a later meal.

Less obnoxious berry lovers include turtles. They spend their time on the ground in the shade of the thicket, waiting for berries to drop. When the blackberries are very ripe they fall from the canes, making a gentle berry rain. Oh, turtles' delight—shuffling from treat to tasty treat!

New Neighbors

A farmer friend of ours has a new neighbor and a not-so-new problem that seems to develop too often in the country.

Some city folks bought a small building lot adjoining Earl's farm. There was a thick old hedgerow growing along the property line. The buyers asked Earl whether he minded if they cut down the hedgerow. Earl explained that the hedgerow was there because it slowed the winds blowing through the valley. He showed them that it was planted on a little rise of land so it would stop runoff from his field in heavy rains. The hedgerow provided shelter for wildlife, and plenty of blackberries, too.

The new neighbor, checking property lines, found that most of the hedgerow was on his lot and bulldozed it away so he would have an unobstructed view of the neighboring farms and twenty extra feet of backyard space.

Earl was sad to see the hedgerow go, but he dug a

drainage swale on his side of the property line to direct field runoff away from the new neighbor, whose house is lower than the field.

In midsummer Earl harvested winter wheat and baled the straw. The new neighbor came to see him and complained about the noise of the tractors late in the evening.

After the harvest, Earl turned his cattle into the stubble of the field and connected his electric fence to keep the livestock contained. The new neighbor came to complain about the possible danger to his children from the electric fence.

Later in the season Earl spread manure on the field in preparation for planting, and the neighbor complained about the odor.

It rained very hard. The neighbor's cellar flooded and he complained.

Earl was born and raised on his farm, and he has grown his living from his land for forty years. The new neighbor wanted to live in the country. He wanted a house with a view of the beautiful, carefully tended farmland around him. Then he wanted the farmer to stop farming because it annoyed him.

If Earl sold his farm and divided it into thirty building lots for houses, the country charm that attracted the new neighbor would be gone. Much more serious, more acres of rich farm land would be taken out of production. Pennsylvania farmland, with its deep, rich soil and abundant water, is some of the best farmland in the world, and it is disappearing fast.

Earl has enlarged the drainage swale and planted new trees along the banks of the wide, shallow ditch. Eventually these trees, with the addition of others planted by birds, will make a new hedgerow. He has moved his electric fence to the inside of the newly planted trees, but he is not going to stop plowing and planting, fertilizing, harvesting, or grazing cattle on his field. Why should he?

Potatoes and Dependencies

Patrick is the family potato grower. In the spring he plants potato eyes in shallow trenches. As they grow he heaps soil and mulch around the potato plants. Hilling potatoes is important because all the new potatoes will form above the eyes.

Last week we dug the potatoes, sorted them, and dried them in the sun. Then we carried them to the bins in the cellar. The ground was dug and turned as we collected the potatoes, and all the mulch that Patrick had used to hill the potatoes was mixed into the soil. Our potato patch is moved each year to a new site where we want to prepare the soil for a garden or nursery bed.

After the potaotes are harvested, I rake and smooth the ex-potato ground. Then, using a four-foot board laid across the bed as a guide, I plant perennial divisions in neat rows six inches apart. Divisions are small pieces of parent plants. Each one has some roots and a crown. Planted out in the late summer, these plantlets develop new roots and buds for growth the following spring. I plant divisions close together because most of them will be dug up and shipped to other gardens early in the spring.

In addition to making and planting divisions for the nursery, I transplant many seedlings. Along the steps from the driveway down to the house, columbines have colonized. In the fall hundreds of columbine seedlings compete for growing room. I lift lots of them and plant them in rows in the nursery. I also transplant seedlings grown in pots. Plants are propagated year-round by various methods, and as soon as we have a bit of prepared ground it is filled.

I keep the records for the nursery business in Hydrangea. Hydrangea is an old tobacco building below the driveway halfway between the house and the barn. It seems to float amid a huge stand of snowball hydrangea bushes, hence its name. Hydrangea is about twelve feet square with many windows and a small stove. It is bright and cozy in winter, and in summer it is open and airy. Under the peaked roof there is a sleeping loft. Hydrangea is the office and the guest room.

We have other small buildings, or dependencies, here. We bought several farm buildings that had fallen into disuse, took them apart, and brought them here. One is now our library. We all love books and can rarely be persuaded to part with even those we have already read. We re-erected one of our bought buildings in a wooded glen and lined the inside with bookshelves.

The library is a favorite rainy day place. There are hundreds of good books, the rain rattles on the tin roof, and a big, old feather-filled couch is divinely comfortable. There is no phone and no electricity in the library, and the building is off in the woods on a lane of its own.

In the shady nursery area up on the hill is The Camp. We owned The Camp for several years before we bought the farm. It was our summer weekend spot. Another bought building was re-erected on the hillside and porches built around it. One porch, looking out into the woods, has an old-fashioned porch swing. At the back of the building there is a solar shower with warm rainwater. On another side, under another porch, is a little kitchen that opens out onto a sunny stone terrace.

The dependencies double our indoor living space, and the distances between the house and these little buildings makes each one a quiet, peaceful retreat.

September Hay

The haymaker, Mr. Traite, was here yesterday with his tractor and mower to cut our hay. He was back today to rake it into rows and turn it over so it will dry evenly in the sun. Tomorrow, if the weather stays sunny and dry, he will bale the hay so we can bring it into the barn.

We took an after-school picnic out to the edge of the hayfield to watch Mr. Traite mow back and forth across the hillside. Many different creatures make their homes in the hayfield. Pheasants flew up in front of the tractor. Other birds and small animals moved into the uncut grass. Finally, only a narrow strip of tall, thick grass stood in the center of the field.

As the tractor and mower advanced, the grassy strip exploded with wildlife. Quail and grouse and young pheasants flew and squawked toward the woods. Rabbits, mice, voles, toads, and snakes zipped across the fresh-cut hay toward the cover of the hedge and the old stone walls around the field.

This is the third cutting from our little hayfield this year. If it does not rain while the hay is drying, we will have enough to feed and bed our sheep, goats, and other animals over the winter.

With good weather and good work, every year the mixed grasses in our hayfield can be mowed and baled in late May, then again around the Fourth of July, and in September. Sometimes, if the spring is late, or the summer is dry, or the haymaker unavailable, one or more cuttings of hay are lost.

Last May, after the hay was mowed, raked, and ready to bale, it rained steadily for three days. The cut hay lying in the field soaking wet began to turn black with fungus. It could not be dried or stored or used by the animals. We picked up the spoiled hay and composted it for the garden. Eventually I was delighted to have such a mountain of mulch for the flowers. But last spring, when it was fine, sweet hay gone soggy and moldy, I wanted to cry.

It is very starry tonight. The sky is absolutely clear and the air is dry. Perfect haymaking weather.

Miles of Vines

The lanes were all overgrown when we moved here. Young trees grew in the roadways, and wild grapevine was entwined in all the trees, large and small. More vines crossed and recrossed the driveway in the trees above. A tangled green tunnel rounded the curve and plunged downhill to the farm. Before a truck or car could get to the farm, miles of vines had to be cut and pulled out of the lane.

Grapevine is as tough as rope and almost as flexible. It grows in a springy tangle. Tendrils, that look like little wooden springs, twist around everything in reach, including each other.

As we began to cut the brush and vines out of the lane, we realized that the grapevines were as bulky and tangled lying on the ground as they had been in the trees. They tripped us constantly. We tried rolling them into big, lumpy balls and putting them on a brush pile. Then, as we tripped and snipped and chopped the rope-like vines, we began to think of uses for them. Wattle fence! Since very primitive times people have woven vines on frames for fencing and even for houses.

We saved all the long pieces of vine that were the thickness of a broomstick. As the vines were pulled out of the treetops, we cut off the side branches and dragged the trimmed vines down the driveway to the barnyard.

We drew a line on the ground to mark the fence line, then drove stakes into the ground, one foot apart, along the line. Carefully we wove the grapevine in and out of the posts.

Long before the lane was completely clear, we had a handsome chicken-yard fence. The wattle fence kept some fat laying hens confined, but it was not really suitable for hard barnyard use.

Young goats climbed it and sheep ate it. Small, spry chickens went right through it. Finally after a heavy, wet spring snow, an avalanche of snow slid off the huge barn roof and squashed it flat! When the snow melted, we cut off the broken stakes and carried the wattle away.

Each day I walk to the end of the lane to get the mail and meet the school bus. I still cut grapevines. Small pencil-thick vines grow from the huge old vine roots, and I harvest them for basket-making.

In summer while the vines are growing, they are soft and water-filled and break easily. By fall some of the plant cells in the vines have become very stringy and tough.

The vines are ripe for harvesting when the school year

begins. Every school day I cut and pull vine from the trees along the lane. During the few minutes that I wait for the school bus, I cut off the tangled side branches. Then we drag the grapevine down the lane to the house as we walk home, like peacocks with twenty-foot tails.

I have quite a lot of grapevine in the yard around the house. It is drying and shrinking in the sun. Soon we will have basket-making weather, and I will use the piles and miles of vines.

Autumn Harvest

Lately I have kept a pair of garden clippers and some string in my pockets. Every plant on the farm is begging to be collected or harvested. Cooler temperatures, with gentle autumn rains and sunshine, have brought out the best in summer flowers and vegetables.

We have picked armloads of flowers to dry for everlasting bouquets. After dinner we sit on the porch and pick off the leaves so the stems and flowers will dry

quickly. Then we bundle the stem ends in rubber bands and hang the flowers upside down in the warm dark of the barn to air dry.

We took away the gourd plant. The leaves had turned gray with mildew, and, though the plant was silvery in the September moonlight, it was downright ugly in the garden. We cut off the gourds, a great pile are ripening in the sun. The huge, hairy leaves of the plant filled the wheelbarrow three times for the trip to the compost heap.

The gourd plant came from the compost that we added to the flower garden last spring. The stowaway seed sprouted when the weather was just right, then grew rapidly. We didn't know whether the seedling would be a gourd or a pumpkin plant, but we knew it would grow to be very large, so we carefully directed the first viny stems away from the flowers and onto the lawn.

From June to September the plant grew. In early morning huge yellow-orange blossoms tipped the vine, and on hot days it seemed to grow before our eyes. Gourds formed, replacing the blossoms. We mowed the grass around the gourd plant, and by Labor Day the plant was about the size of a living room and studded with round, softball-size gourds.

The gourd plant was a bonus from the compost heap. Many of our garden treasures have been volunteers. What a lovely present the jump-up gourd plant was! It grew enough gourds for the whole second grade.

Deer

We were walking home from the school bus stop today when eleven deer crossed the driveway right in front of us. As we rounded the curve, the first deer came out of the bramble thicket, bounding onto the gravel drive and downhill into the woods. She was followed by ten more deer, does and fawns, that raced down the bank, across the drive, and into the poplar grove. We could see their muscles bunch and stretch under their thick coats, and we could see the veins in their big antenna-like ears.

As we watched, the deer seemed to melt into the woods, disappearing quickly in the light and shadow of the trees. The splashy colors of the leaves provided excellent camouflage. The sound of their passing could be heard after they were out of sight. I am sure we surprised the deer, but I don't think we frightened them.

It was a thrill to see a herd of deer close at hand. They flowed across our path as gracefully as water.

Basket Weather

When we were city dwellers, the weather was either pleasant or awful, but we did not think about it much. Here at the farm the weather affects almost eveything we do.

It has been raining for days! We are having the kind of soggy weather that strips the last of the fall leaves from the trees. It rained hard for a day, then settled in to a gentle, misty shower. I am delighted with this rain. I have been looking forward to it. It is basket weather.

All the vines that I have collected this fall are soaked. They have had time to shrink and ripen in the sun, and now they are wet, flexible, and ready to weave. Basket materials—vine, cane, wood splits, or straw—have to be flexible. When the fibers are wet, they can be bent around the basket spokes and even folded back on themselves. Later, when the fibers dry out again, they will become stiff and hold their shape in the basket.

The rainy weather has prepared the vine, and the high humidity keeps it damp and flexible while it is worked. All this wetting can be done in a sink or bathtub, or the work can be kept damp with wet towels, but a three-day rain is ideal for basket-making.

I clear almost everything off the porch to work on baskets. The long pieces of vine get flapped around as I turn the work in my hands. I have knocked over plants, coffee cups—even kittens—when I did not clear the area before beginning.

The spokes of the basket form the frame, and the weavers fill in around the spokes. Any tough, stringy plant can be used for basket making. I use grapevine, honeysuckle, grasses, mint stems, yucca leaves, iris leaves, and birch twigs for weavers. The spokes must be very strong and flexible. Honeysuckle is wonderful for this.

In its first stage a basket looks like a big star made of sticks, or perhaps like a spider. The sticks, or spokes, are bound together in the middle with a thin vine; then the weaving begins. The stick-star of spokes is slippery and hard to hang onto, but as the weavers are passed under one spoke and over the next, a firm basket bottom, easier to grip, takes shape. When the bottom is the desired size, the spokes are bent gently upward to make the sides. Once the corner is turned, the rest is a simple matter of over-and-under weaving until the basket is big enough.

After an hour's soaking, the basket spokes are bent over and tucked in to make the top edge. A length of stout vine forms the handle. Both ends are cut on an angle, then

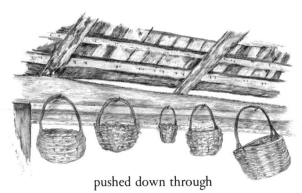

pushed down through
the basket beside two opposite spokes.
The handle can be bound to the basket with thin vine.

Hanging from the porch rafters is an assortment of
baskets. I buy and trade baskets, as well as making them.
I use them all. There are egg baskets, berry baskets, and
carrier baskets. We have one basket with a lid that is our
bunny basket; we use it to carry bunnies to school for
classroom visits.

Baskets are strong and lightweight and allow light and air
to pass through their sides. They are almost unbreakable
and extremely useful. Once a year I put all my small
baskets into my mother-in-law's dishwasher, without soap.
The washing and steaming cleans them and restores
moisture to the dried-out baskets, strengthening them.

I sit on the porch and weave the soggy afternoon away.
I can watch the ducks waddling happily in the puddles
between the barnyard and the stream. The rain has given
the trees and plants a good long drink of water to help
them through the winter, and it has given me basket
weather.

Getting Ready for Winter

It snowed a little last night. In the morning the weeping cherry tree that grows by the stream was especially beautiful. Each drooping black branch was capped with white, and the last leaves, golden yellow, hung down fluttering in the wind.

The last summer flowers, green and blossoming yesterday, now look like cooked spinach. The water inside of each tiny plant cell froze and expanded, breaking the cell walls. When the sun came out in the morning, the ice melted and the plants collapsed.

Some plants die after a frost. Some die back to their roots. Some lose their leaves, and some are evergreen, but most plants will be leafless from now until spring.

Spring is a long way off, though, and now there are plenty of jobs to do to get ready for winter, which is just around the corner. Today our getting-ready jobs included gathering firewood, which we have been doing on every

97

dry day lately.

We collect only dead wood. Live or green wood must be dried for a year, sometimes two, before it makes really good firewood because it is full of water or sap.

Our tractor is the heart of the firewood operation. Patrick had a bucksaw made. Its steel frame is bolted to the tractor, and the large and toothy saw blade is powered by the tractor via a belt. Behind the sawbuck is a cart to carry wood, workers, tools, a chainsaw, and a pot of tea. We make a noisy parade along one of the old lanes that crisscross this hillside. Sandy dog follows behind, preferring not to ride.

With the chain saw, dead trees are cut into manageable sizes and carried to the sawbuck on the tractor. Small windfalls, the branches blown down by the wind, are picked up, broken into short lengths, and thrown into the cart.

When we've gathered a big pile, the tractor is started, the bucksaw put into gear, and the poles and logs are lifted onto the buck, or cradle, of the saw and cut into chunks for our stoves.

Saws of all kinds are terrifically dangerous. Only one adult, the sawyer, stays anywhere near the bucksaw on the tractor when it is cutting. When the wood is all cut, the saw is taken out of gear and its big, round, spinning blade moves slower, then stops. The tractor is shut off and quiet is turned on.

We throw all the cut wood into the cart on top of the sticks, then we hop on top of the load for the ride home.

It takes two people about an hour to cut a cartload of wood. At the same time, they have tidied up a small area of the forest floor and had plenty of fresh air and exercise.

We pile our wood around the trunk of the huge spruce tree in front of the house. We stack it neatly and carefully so that it will stay dry and so it will not fall and hurt someone. That woodpile sits right in front of the door from October until May. It is fine to look at it, big and well-stacked, and know that it will keep us cozy and warm for the cold months to come.

The broken-up sticks from the cart go under the porch, completely out of the weather. These dry sticks are important. They are kindling, the small dry wood used to start the fire in the stove. Once winter comes, any sticks in the woods will get soaking wet or be covered with snow, so a good supply is collected and stored on dry fall days.

Today, when the cart was empty, we used the handy old tractor and cart to haul the porch windows from summer storage in the barn to the house. These big windows fit around the porch, completely enclosing it for the winter. They are heavy and awkward to handle, but it is a worthwile effort. The enclosed porch becomes a windless suntrap, often warmer than the inside of the house on a sunny winter day.

The winter view from the porch is longer than the summer view because the trees are bare. We can see reflected sunlight twinkling on the pond in the valley, and the houses on the far hills are like tiny toys in the landscape.

Seedy Season

Last night we heard a scratchy sound from upstairs where the big bed stands against the wall. We went upstairs and looked carefully under the bed with a flashlight. The scratching sound stopped, and there was no sign of a mouse or any of the trashy bits a mouse leaves behind.

We gave up the search; but when we were back downstairs, the noise started overhead again. This time, when we stuck our heads under the bed, we noticed a wrinkle in the large, heavy rug that covers most of the bedroom floor. We moved the bed and were turning the rug back when out dashed a little white-footed mouse. It disappeared from sight as we bumbled with the rug.

The mouse had left behind a collection of rug fuzz, nut shells, a few seeds, and plenty of mouse manure along the rug-wrinkle tunnel. Ugh!

By this time of year in the woods, thousands of

small animals have made snug winter homes and food storerooms under the leaf carpet. The little four-foots have collected nuts and grain, seeds and berries for a winter food supply. Some small animal harvesters are very efficient workers. Others work hard but are rather silly and forgetful about the location of their pantries, and some would rather rob another animal's storeroom than collect provisions for themselves.

Groundhogs wear their pantries under their skins. As the days grow shorter, groundhogs earn their name as they hog up food until they are so full and fat they can scarely move. Then they shuffle off to their burrows and sleep until spring. During the winter their bodies use the stored fat layer.

Small animals, by collecting and storing food, spread seeds around and plant new trees and bushes. I don't know where the mouse under the rug has moved, but I hope it is outside under the leaves, planting seeds with its relatives.

From the doorway I can watch squirrels eating the bright red fruits that enclose the dogwood seeds. Other squirrels are up in the spruce tree stripping the cones and sending down a rain of little wooden scales. The bush honeysuckles are covered with small red berries, every one of which the birds will pick off and eat before the first of the year.

We walked down to the bottom of the hill where the winterberry holly grows along a drainage ditch. These deciduous hollies are very ordinary-looking in summer; but in the fall, stripped of their leaves, their twiggy shapes are interesting and their red fruit glorious. We will do some berry collecting just before Christmas, using the bright winterberry holly and delicate red rosehips to decorate our wreaths.

When we came home from our walk we were covered with flat triangles, hooked feathers, and round balls. As we sat on the porch picking off the seeds that had hitched rides on our sweaters and jeans, Sandy dog combed burs from her fat, hairy tail. Some of the cats in the barnyard were busy with the same job.

Burdocks, bur cucumbers, tick seeds, stick tights, and begger's ticks are all weed seeds, packaged to travel. Too heavy to fly, and not as tasty as other kinds of seeds, these opportunists have hooks! They attach themselves to any fur or cloth that brushes against them. The dry, leafless parent plants stand holding their seeds, waiting for a passing animal to collect and distribute them.

Almost Christmas

Our daily walks have become quests for the perfect Christmas tree. Pierre prefers Virginia junipers or the red cedars that grow at the bottom of the hill. Deer browse on the cedars, nibbling the branch tips and causing them to branch again and again. They are columnar and thick and have a tangy smell—good qualities for our small house. We tied a red handkerchief on one especially nice cedar tree. We'll look some more before we cut our tree, but we'll be able to find this cedar again, even if it snows.

My Christmas tree vote goes to a small fat spruce that is growing out of the stone wall at the edge of the hay field. The tree is in a bad place and will have to be cut down soon. If we don't choose it for Christmas this year, I will shear it, imitating the deer. New growth will be tight and thick, making the spruce a worthier candidate next year.

Patrick favors the Virginia pines that grow near the road at the top of the hill. They are bright green with open, airy branches. Several of the young ones are Christmas tree size.

As we have been looking for a Christmas tree, we have been pruning some of the evergreens. We save these pruning jobs until this time of the year so we can use the cut branches for Christmas wreaths. The branches are carried back to the top of the barn where I make wreaths on my work tables.

Our wreath-making is for home decoration, fun, and profit. We sell wreaths at the local farmers' market, and we also make a number of them for friends. Each wreath must be beautiful and absolutely fresh.

As Christmas gets closer, I spend more and more time in the barn working. Patrick and Pierre help with gathering the greens, but I do the wreath making. They keep me supplied with hot coffee and encouragement, and they deliver the finished products.

The last wreaths are for our house and barn doors. Then I sweep out the workroom, and we make a sweet-smelling bonfire of all the thick, bare branches and leftover bits.

Soon we'll cut our Christmas tree and drag it home. We'll put colored lights around the porch and hang up our own wreaths. The farm is snow-covered and beautiful. It's almost Christmas and we're almost ready.

Oh Possum

Have you ever heard the expression, "playing possum?" An opossum plays it very well. He simply flops down on the ground and plays dead. He is so convincing that his enemies—people or dogs—are fooled and leave the creature alone.

Last night Patrick's daughter, Marie, here for a holiday visit, went out to the barn to say goodnight to the cats and kittens. She burst back into the house looking alarmed. "There is a big dead animal right by the steps!"

We grabbed a flashlight and all ran out the door to look.

There in the snow at the bottom of the stone steps lay a large gray possum. Its long, hairless tail was wrapped around its belly and its mouth was open, its tongue lolling out on the snow.

The creature was perfectly still. Sandy dog came down from her snug place on the porch to investigate. She sniffed the possum, and pushed it with her paw. Then she walked back to her warm bed with no further interest in the animal.

We went inside, too. If the possum was dead, we could not do anything about him, and if he was not dead, he soon would be if he had to stay still on the frozen ground for too long. We kept an eye on the possum through the window, and after a few minutes of quiet, the creature got up, shook itself, and hurried off toward the woods. It was our first encounter with a possum "playing possum."

Snowflakes

Winter arrived here last week. First it snowed a thick layer that blocked the driveway. Then it got extremely cold and windy. Everything was frozen hard. It snowed and blew some more, and now the sun is out and the farm is transformed by a blanket of glittering white.

While it was still snowing, Pierre and I looked at snowflakes with a magnifying glass. We put a metal tray out on the porch to get it very cold, then we caught snowflakes on the cold surface and looked at them with our small hand lenses. On the cold tray the snowflakes lasted long enough for us to get a good look before they melted to tiny specks of water. We saw for ourselves that each snowflake really is a six-sided crystal, and each lovely little snowflake is different from all the others.

All the animals' drinking water freezes during the night. In the morning we carry kettles of hot water to the barnyard. We pour the hot water over the frozen buckets and knock out the ice lumps. The cats, chickens, and ducks watch as we refill the waterers with clean, warm water. Then they all gather to drink together while the water is warm. The sheep and goats take good long drinks of water in the barn before they go out for the day.

The water bucket in the field is useless, because it freezes so quickly.

After a few days of melting and knocking out ice from the barnyard containers, we had quite a lot of odd-shaped, oversize ice cubes. Pierre put them on his sled and hauled them to a frozen rain barrel, where he piled them into an ice sculpture.

He adds more lumps as they freeze, and the water dripping from the roof above has fused the ice cubes together and added some icicles.

It is snowing again tonight.

February Snow

Groundhog Day has come and gone. The groundhog would have been crazy to come out on such a vile day. It rained and snowed, and if the groundhog had come out he probably would have slipped on the ice-covered snow and fallen flat on his face.

The snow got deep and drifted during the last few weeks. We can walk on top of it now because it has a solid crust of ice. It is a strange change of perspective to see the world from two feet above normal eye level.

There is a huge snowdrift at the mailbox. The snow there is about eight feet deep. We cut steps in the snowbank going down to the mailbox and the plowed road. The mailbox is covered with snow, and only its front door is visible in the wall of white.

The sheep and goats have not been let out in the field for a while. The snow is too deep and the wind too cold. They stay in the barn with the doors open to the south-facing barnyard. Under the eight-foot overhang there is no snow. The sheep and goats sun themselves there and chew their hay. The sheep enjoy the snow, they plow through it and kick and buck and dance in it. Our goats do not like snow at all. They sort of test it, then avoid it.

All of our regular routes around the farm are tramped out in a network of narrow paths through the snow. With each new layer of snow the trails become deeper.

We have terrific sledding on the sloping driveways, which are too snow-filled for cars. We have long, rectangular plastic sleds that are important transportation and enormous fun. We load groceries or a hundred-pound bag of feed onto one of the sleds, jump on and ride right down to the barnyard gate or the door of the house.

The walk uphill to the car, road, or school bus is not fast, but it is interesting. The snow is full of tracks. There are bird tracks in neat little pairs and rabbit tracks that look huge because the rabbit hops along, landing on all four feet together and making one large print. We have seen some very odd patterns on the snow. One was the track of a pine cone that was rolled along by the wind, leaving checkered marks. We have also spotted mouse tunnels through the snow and a funny little set of footprints made by a mouse that traveled in scallops. Deer seem to use our paths, then branch off into the woods.

Today the sun was out bright and strong. We moved the thermometer about a foot, from the shade of the porch post into the sunshine, and the temperature rose from thirty-five to sixty-four degrees. Spring is not far off now.

Winter Work

The snow has melted in patches. On the south side of trees and on the steepest south-facing hillsides, a few sun-favored spots are clear of snow. There are groups of small, round holes in the snow under the big walnut tree. At the bottom of each hole are the tips of daffodil leaves. As they push up through the soil and out of the ground, the growing leaves create a little heat and melt the snow cover.

Along the path of the stream bubbling downhill from the house, watercress is starting to grow. The cold spring water is warmer than the air. The stream bed is a little microclimate of its own, thawed and fertile.

Each fall I think winter will be very long and dull, but the time always rushes past, and before the winter work is done, spring arrives.

When the days are wet or very cold, I do inside jobs. I have whitewashed the inside of the house from attic to springhouse.

It is a good winter job. All the lively brushing keeps me warm. This old house must have hundreds of coats of whitewash on its stone walls, splashed and brushed on every year or so to whiten and clean them.

To make whitewash, special lime is mixed with water, and allowed to sit, overnight at least, but longer is better. Then the whitewash is painted on with a huge, long-bristled brush. While the wall is wet, it looks terrible, but once it is dry it is shining white and fresh.

When the whitewashing is done, I oil the woodwork. Over time, wood dries out and needs to have oils added to preserve its strength and beauty. The floors, stairs, and wood paneling get a good soak of turpentine and linseed oil.

Turpentine is the carrier that makes it possible for the wood to absorb the linseed oil quickly. The turpentine-linseed oil mixture has a strong, clean smell. As it feeds and beautifies, it kills insects that are living in the wood. The mixture is brushed on, allowed to soak in, then rubbed with a rag until the surface is dry. Midway through February the house positively sparkles!

We were extremely cold our first winter in the country. As soon as we left the side of the stove we shivered and rushed right back, but still we were hardly ever warm. For some reason it did not occur to us to get moving to get warm. Now, if I am feeling chilly, I put on a hat, coat, and boots and go outside and do something, even if it is just taking a walk, and soon, no matter how cold it is outside, I am warm in body and spirit. Winters, since that first cold one, have been busy and productive. We have been warmer, healthier, and happier.

New Field

I was very excited when we had the new nursery field plowed because I had waited four years for it.

First it had a serious weed problem, so we plowed it several times and pulled out roots. We grew vegetables on part of it with excellent results. The second year the field was flooded. Our first year had been exceptionally dry, but the next year we had normal weather, and the low garden paths ran with water all summer. We dug ditches across the field toward the stream to drain away the water, but it was still very wet.

We contacted the Soil Conservation Service in our county, and a woman came out to look at our problem. She laid out a drain plan. Following her suggestions, we hired an excavating firm to dig a ditch and install slotted pipe deep in the field. The digger started at the stream and moved uphill.

Near the top of the field he hit water! The whole long ditch rushed with water for a while, then settled down to a steady flow. Some side branches from the drainage ditch were dug, piped, and connected. Along one of the branch ditches, the huge bulldozer sank into the ground. The surface had looked perfectly normal, but it was so wet that it could not support the weight of the huge machine. The bulldozer operator freed his machine, dug some more, and uncovered another spring. More slotted pipe was laid, the ditches were partly filled with crushed stone, and the soil was pushed back in. The drain has been pouring two gallons of water per minute into the stream ever since.

After the drains were installed last April, the field was a muddy, rough-surfaced mess. We sowed Sudan grass on it and waited. By early summer the field was dry. In the fall we plowed under the Sudan grass and replanted, this time with winter rye. These grass cover crops smother weeds, and repeated plowing pulls out troublesome weed roots. Later, the grasses rot, and their remains improve the tilth, or texture, of the soil.

Now the rye grass has been plowed under, and this spring the ground will be ready to plant. We will use this field intensively, and, once it has been shoveled into raised beds four feet wide, it will not be plowed again for many years.

We will work from the paths between the beds, planting, weeding, and harvesting the plants we grow to sell. Then we will add compost to renew the soil and plant the raised beds again.

The additional land under cultivation will double the size of our nursery ground. The established areas are well in hand, and we should be able to cope with the increased workload of the new field.

Fire of Spring

Throughout the past winter we cut down trees and brush to enlarge the pasture. All of the large branches and tree trunks that we could use for firewood we stacked to dry and season. Debris from the treetops and shrubs was dragged to the middle of the pasture. It made a mountain of densely packed brush.

A few days ago, after three days of hard rain, we called our local Volunteer Fire Department to let them know we were going to burn the pile. The Fire Department likes to know about a controlled fire before they get reports of smoke or fire.

The weather was perfect; there was no wind at all. Everything, including our huge burn pile, was soaking wet. The wetter the better because once a pile begins to burn, it dries itself, and if the surrounding area is wet enough, there is very little danger of the fire spreading or of flying ash lighting another fire.

We lit the burn pile right after breakfast and spent the entire day tending the fire. When the great bulk of the brush had burned, we carried out all the rotten wood, old dog bedding, hopelessly broken chairs, and any other burnable trash that had accumulated over the past months.

Late in the afternoon I poked some nice big potatoes into the embers and raked glowing coals around a pot of homemade soup. We ate our supper in the pasture, warmed by the last glow of the great burn pile. A delicate new moon swam across the sky, and Patrick reminded us that it was March twenty-first, the vernal equinox. The bonfire was a fitting tribute to the end of winter and the coming of spring, with all its marvelous potential.

Today I stopped at a tulip poplar tree, leaned my back against its trunk, and looked up. I like to measure myself against a tree. It reminds me that humans are very small in the whole scheme of things.

Once I am measured and have reflected on my size and place in the universe, I marvel at the tulip poplar tree. Its trunk is very tall and straight, with smooth, black bark. As it grows, the tulip poplar sheds its lower branches, keeping only a light, twiggy crown at the top. And, best of all, each twig is tipped with a tiny wooden candle, silhouetted against the sky. These seed heads decorate the tree. Then, as they dry, they come apart, and the seeds, each encased in a tiny wooden helicopter, glide and spin to the ground.

We, as the stewards of this land, have accepted the responsibility for seeing that the seeds will fall on fertile ground.

About the Author

Farmer, gardener, teacher, writer, wife, and mother, but not necessarily in that order, Jane Reed Lennon has gardened in the United States, England, France, Switzerland, and Morocco, gathered a prairie plant collection in Colorado for the Wright-Ingraham Institute, and helped develop a community gardening program called Philadelphia Green which has become the national model for such programs.

Text set in Janson Dutch typefaces and final mechanicals prepared by Action Comp Co., Inc. of Baltimore, Maryland.

Printed on Warren acid-free seventy pound Olde Style paper, smythe-sewn and casebound by John D. Lucas Printing Company of Baltimore, Maryland.